Chance Meetings

Chance Meetings

Published by Poetry Space Ltd. 2014

© Poems: Roger Elkin

© Cover photograph: Chris Sims

This edition first published in Great Britain in 2014
by Poetry Space Ltd.

Poetry Space Ltd. Company No. 7144469.

Reg.office. 21 Davis Close, Barrs Court, Bristol, BS30 7BU

Printed and bound in Great Britain
by Whitehall Printing Ltd.

ISBN 978-1-909404-11-3

www.poetryspace.co.uk

Chance Meetings

Roger Elkin

poetryspace

Prize-winning poet, Roger Elkin was literary advisor to the Leek Arts Festival for whom he organized an International Poetry Competition (1982-1992); the co-Editor (1985-1988) of *Prospice*, the international literary quarterly, issues 17-25 inclusive; and sole Editor (1991-2006), of *Envoi*, poetry magazine, issues 101-145 inclusive.

He has reviewed for *Stand, Outposts*, and *Envoi*; and was poetry tutor on residential weekend courses at Wedgwood College, Barlaston.

He is available for book-signings, readings, writing workshops and poetry competition adjudication: contact eiger@hotmail.co.uk for further details.

Other Publications by Roger Elkin include:

Poetry:

Pricking Out	*Aquila*,	1988
Points of Reference	*Headland*,	1996
Home Ground	*Headland*,	2002
Rites of Passing	*Shoestring*,	2006
Blood Brothers, New & Selected Poems	*Headland*,	2006
No Laughing Matter	*Cinnamon Press*,	2007
Dog's Eye View	*Lapwing Press*,	2010
Fixing Things	*Indigo Dreams*,	2011
Bird in Hand	*Indigo Dreams*,	2012
Marking Time	*Sentinel Poetry Movement*,	2013

Prose:

Critical articles on Ted Hughes's **Recklings** poems in Keith Sagar, **The Challenge of Ted Hughes**, *(St Martin's Press, 1995);* Joanny Moulin, **Lire Ted Hughes**, *(Edition du Temps, 1999)*; and on **The Ted Hughes Society** and **Earth-moon Ted Hughes** websites.

Travel, in the younger sort, is a part of education; in the elder, a part of experience.

Francis Bacon, **Essays,** *18:* **Of Travel**

Acknowledgements

are due to the editors of the following various magazines and anthologies in which earlier versions of some of these poems have appeared:

For Rhino in a Shrinking World; Onward: A Literary Anthology; **Mermaids Off Cromer Pier & Other Poems; Poetry on the Lake:** *Hortus Conclusus;* **Sentinel Champions 8**; The Partners Annual Open Poetry Competition Awards Magazine, 2010; Tips for Writers 81; **This is a book about Alice.**

The following poems have been awarded places in Open Poetry Competitions:

At the end of the day	**HC Poetry on the Lake**	2009
African Wild Dogs	**HC Fylde Writers**	2012
More than Orange	**HC Swale Life**	2012
Mustapha Loves Her	**HC Gregory O' Donoghue**	2011
Odd Jobbing Thomas	**HC Sentinel Literary Quarterly**	2011
Shooting Rhino	**1st Prize, Southport**	2011
Understanding Dung Beetles	**1st Prize, Build Africa**	2012
Vultures	**1st Prize, Theatre Royal, Onward**	2010
Zulu Dancing	**1st Prize, Earlyworks Press**	2012

For Eileen

for whom I go to the ends of the earth

Contents

Turkish Delights

Chance Meetings

Turkish Delights

High Flier

Thirty-eight thousand feet
above ground-level. Clouds so near
I could lean out to touch them.
Would they be wet, and cold?

From above there's archipelagos and atolls
shining like sunlit polar landscapes;
or vaster plateaus mirroring the rhythms of the land
miles below with valleys, hills, rolling forests, dales:

either way, a massive landscape
carved in shades of white and folding away
beneath vastnesses of clear skies.

Suddenly, there's a cloud-gash
revealing thousands of feet underneath
fields patchworking like my son's camouflaged pants
and rivers glistening their snail-trails in silver sunlight

and I'm overawed with the birdness of things ...

And, as suddenly, the play of light
casts a cloud-shadow like a palm-stain louring over the land

and I understand the retraction of antlers
                    the pillings of skin
                    the shivering fear of stabbing beak
                                        squelching step
                                        slashing knife

the snailness of things ...

You Round the Corner

and there he is
this gardener in his wild-anchusa-blue overalls
looming from the oil-glinting shields of laurel leaves
and the coin-dull oleanders brightening ever-so slightly
under the Turkish April sun.

He's as surprised as you are, so stops just short of
turning heel, and in a sort of one-two-step tribal dance squares full
on, his eyes shading through veiled glazing alarm to calm, till lighting up
wide and blackbird-bright, as if he knows you,

but all the time
he's ransacking his mind trying to fix a name to looks, his face
avalanching into ease, his brows drowning out their frowns, and lips
filling into a grin that works his smile like a glove-puppet.

Meanwhile you're negotiating
the space between you – two paces forward, then back – your mind
piecing together face-frames you've seen in films and magazines:
that Amerindian-Bolivian-mix with chiselled cheekbones,
grizzled jaw under bandit-shadow stubble, a sort of gypsy-bristling
on chin – walnut wrinkling skin – slashing black moustache –
eyebrows to match – cross between Charles Bronson and Saddam Hussein –
that peasant handsomeness with oryx eyes so beautiful you'd die for.

This far it's taken a minimum of speech. You haven't his language,
so the shrugs and grunts, the shoulder-lifts, eye-smiles, body-signs
have bridged the silences between you – and before you know it
you're shaking his outstretched hand, and, crossing the gateway with
its diamond-spangled wire, have begun drifting through the gardens as
if long-time friends – but cannot resist your suspicions.

Money, must be money that he's after.

You've seen this before: at Luxor with Captain Shakespeare
whose stabbing-daggery eyes sized you up in a single head-to-foot
sliding swipe, then eased into that same beguiling smile,
one hand hitching up his galabeya, the other seeking baksheesh –
so you're convinced you know what this one's up to seconds before
he does – instance the trapped-mouse way he zigzags flowerbeds
as if in search of escape-route – and pinch – the pink flush of rose
is pushed with its hum of colour to your face, him smiling teeth-whitely.

But it's you he's ambushing, playing you out like some trapped animal
with all the skill of his old-man guile, cornering you in the intensity
of generosity, knowing you're helpless, have nothing to return,
this garden his controlling hold.

        And suddenly his arms lift to mimic flight
and, tipping, swing to aeroplane – *Go haus. U tek* – and he's imitating
digging up this scarlet dianthus with its harlot eyes, and next
a gazania with its clashes of amber and jazzy golds – *And theez* –
a finger-snipped tip of herb he's rubbing with his thumb, then pushing
– *Eez gud. U tek haus* – insisting that you sniff.

        Your brain somersaults, grasping at words –
Basil? Marjoram? Oregano? – to salvage this disaster and hoping
that the barrage of unfamiliar sounds will buy you thinking time.
But without realizing you've dipped into your pocket and unscrolled
a roll of Euro notes – *For the rose. The rose. Must go now go* –

        And - *no, no,* NO – he's blackbird crackerjacking,
No pay - eyes flashing in a sort of stamping, hands turning down the cash
and you feel three feet small, wrecked by pettiness, would like to melt
to nothingness. But cannot escape.

To resurrect yourself needs your Vivitar digital camera,
something you're sure he cannot have seen before.
And placing him to take his photograph – *Please here* – insist he rests
his resisting frame against this grapefruit tree with its dusty orbs
lemoning through acid green leaves. Something vulnerable suddenly
comes over him, and he's reduced to your granddad's
generation – back sixty years in half a minute – little old man, grounded
with all the alarm of wounded blackbird, losing face in the face
of the unknown, a sort of defeated weakness that knows no relief
even when you show his pose as preview, and he's that discomposed
he doesn't even know himself, has collapsed to shambling handy-man.

And you have earned your exit-line –
you with your snipped pink rose, your marjoram,
and memory of those vanquished eyes ...

Tulips

for Ramazan

Don't suppose for a moment when you're stuck
in front of your VDU logged onto programs to improve
your English, you give a thought to tulips …

Concerned about your future working at Chamyuva's
five-star *Fantasia Hotel*, why should you turn a hair
at reading that "tulip" has its roots in the Turkish for turban …

Worrying how to make ends meet on your waiter's wages
why bother that seventeenth century Dutch traders
bankrupted themselves paying £400 per bulb in the Tulip Wars …

And planning your family in your cramped Antalya flat
why should you give a fig that Hockney in his Los Angeles hangings
of autobiographical paintings uses the tulip as trademark

And yet, passing on work-days from the Hotel's digs into town
and noting the central reservation flowerbeds rippling with tulip-reds,
you query their being in a place geared-up for holidaying English

then remember the folk-tale of how a Persian prince, learning that his love
was dead, had hurled himself from a cliff-top, and, where his body lay
splintered, there blood-red tulips grew …

Tonight, looking to your future, you'll search his story out
and read it to your first-born son –
haltingly, in English …

Mustapha loves her

I know it right from how his gazelle-sad eyes
light up when first he sets his startled sight on her. *Leddy*
hev lavly herr he says, his fingers lifting – oh so slightly –
as though he hasn't any time to lose possessing her.

Mustapha loves her.

I can tell it from the way he unflaps his red-checked
hamman-mat across the marble massage-slab, then gestures
with welcoming smiles and palms – a sweeping, open glide –
inviting her to place herself face down. *Pleez leddy. Pleez.*

He loves her. The practised manner in which he peels away
her towel revealing thighs cheese-white nearly as his smiling-teeth
convinces me. Not to mention his spine-climbing hands,
fingers circling rhythmically, the shoulder-rollings, palms
snake-laddering up/down up/down her neck, thumbs mussing
through her curls. Hands spidering her arms, her limbs.

He loves her. This I know. The persuasive way he turns
her, slowly lifts her breasts, lingers, moulds them, his fingers
boldly folding over her glistening skin as he works the oilings in.
The lemon scent. The rolls. The swipes. Caresses. Folds.

He loves her. His almond hands glancing across her abdomen
with lifting, easing, stroking gentleness. Strong. Long. Light.
The breaths he takes, sighs she makes eliding with his sibilance,
conspiring at her ear, *Eez okay leddy. Eez okay.*

Mustapha loves her. Pampers her with ceremonies of
sugared apple tea in clear glass cups – *Eez gud* –
his soft brown eyes dispelling uncertainties,
then tresses – gently, gently – his dressing gown
around her glowing shoulders. *Rast pleez. Leddy rast.*

Mustapha loves her. Is sure she'll return for more.

But when the boss-man suddenly appears, eyes as bland
as sesame seed, how Mustapha scuttles like a flustered buck,
his hands hanging daftly, his olive limbs cringing,
his presence melting to anonymities of hamman-lad.

And she is mine. All mine. My wife. Again.

Chance Meetings

Room Staff,
Amazulu Lodge *St. Lucia, S Africa*

Heads in matching bandanas
to their cream, tan and black overalls,
they gather each morning
under the big fig tree.

Have their own-named grey buckets,
with brushes, cloths and mops,
and, waiting for rooms to be vacated,
stand like antelope sheltering
against rain.

How they must envy us our life

      holidaying in twin en-suite rooms
      bigger and more luxuriously equipped
      than their family homes

      our luggage holding more
      than their entire possessions

      and our wide horizons
      mapped by greed.

African Market Traders, Their Craft

Sitting stalled behind salients of fruit and veg –
    asparagus spears, pineapple grenades,
    pomegranates charged with shotted seed –
it's the Mamas that have the commanding site.
Blacks don't frequent here, so prices are high,
writ big in red: for certain, greed isn't in any
way to be compromised by need.

                    Behind them,
pitch on pitch at level of feet, the native crafts –
that mix of kitschy Africa so regular it could be
factory-made: brigades of soapstone rhinos, hippos,
crocs, giraffes; regiments of child-size assegais and
shields; batteries of tribal wooden masks; files of
graded boxes; rounds of bowls; bandoliers of beads.

And, suddenly, they appear, the standing army
of front-line sellers, magicking out of half-light
to loom by our side, where, knowing we English
aren't good at bartering, begin the attack, insisting
Give you good price, their faces widely smiling,
till we put back in place – *Just looking* – the pieces
we've picked out. Then they become lugubrious
and drop their lips, their eyes turning behind them
to the backs of pitches where in places no bigger
than family catacombs they bring up their infantry
in a second offensive, faces spearing the half-dark:
Ma kids. Needing food. I give you good price.

And, before we've realised, we've dropped our guard,
and, proffering rands, become hostage to necessities.

Odd Jobbing Thomas

Arrives early, so before we pull the blinds
he's installed, black bin-liner in hand,
picking up the shields of fig leaves
that have fallen overnight. Wind and rain
and the conspiracy of sap with season
guarantee this ritual – leaf, and twig,
and a brush and shovel to do the steps.

It's a job: not paying well, but he gets
his bellyful of leftover guest-breakfast
like the rest of the staff. And needs
this perk: his T-shirt ripped, trousers
stained, and shoes a flapping disaster
of black leather strapped with wire.

After leaves, it's clearing the boma fire.
Makes it last for half an hour. Or more:
sweeping ash, picking clinker, saving
kindling, piling the tiny pyre ready
for the twilight lighting, then in case
of rain placing the iron-cast lid over
its confining ring of smoke-lipped brick.

Then general watering, snaking the black
hose through massy ferns, spider plants,
tradescantia, and agapanthus, and spraying
fine rainbows – everywhere – even on
the shoes I've left outside to dry.
Sir, am sorree his head bending, a gleam
of fear in his eyes despite my smile.

He can have the shoes when I leave.

Cultural Tour

not Shakaland's film-set replica
of Zulu kraal, thatch everywhere,
circular huts in pecking order in
that traditional balance now just
two stars away from Theme Park

> but higgledy-piggledy
> settlement of wooden uprights
> filled with boulders,
> or fired dung-bricks, then
> roofed with corrugated tin,
> and gaudy paintwork
> daubed to show ownership

not the listless, bored groups of men
paced out, ready to demonstrate
Zulu traditional life, springing into
action as if on cue, and picking up
their smiles, but not in their eyes

> but the folk in their garden-
> fields engaged in that
> stooping rhythm of dib, plant,
> heel – dib, plant, heel –
> that meaningful absorption
> in the process of living a life

not the larger than life Zulu guide – cross
between Forsyth and Lenny Henry –
interspersing his tour with TV jokes,
film gags and innuendo, playing
all the time to the Western girls

> but Ngomo, our driver, who
> fills us with facts/figures;

answers our probing questions,
and smiles emphathetically
at our obvious un-ease – true
ambassador for our learning needs, our care

not the frenetic energetic tribal dancing,
set as in King Shaka's court, each Zulu
trying to out-do the rest against the pounding
of the drum, the chanting – knowing
well enough we couldn't do it for kingdoms

> but a one-step, two-step
> swing from kids,
> girls first, then lads, then all
> in turn and singing out
> the names of things – face,
> elbows, nose, fingers, toes –
> in English, and welcoming us to join in

not the gaggle of village children
hanging around to sell their wares –
beads, jewellery, wire bowls –
strategically placed by the guest restaurant,
their elders lurking in shadows

> but the class of children at the crèche
> that clung to our legs,
> held hands and laughed when
> we proffered sweets,
> marshmallows and pens – and
> up-front their teacher-friend
> enjoying innocent fun

not the fiction of the imagined past

> but the fact of the actual,
> the now

Pharmacy Visit

The four of us squatting on rush-matting
with Ngomo, the doorway a tooth of light,
windows blacked out with bags and sacks, and
hangings curtaining the hut's encircling wall.

Suddenly the room falls dark, a dishevelled figure –
shawled and head-dressed with feathery rags,
sunlight making apricot the muscle toned dark limbs –
enters, sits cross-legged opposite, no eye contact,
bends in a cat-like curve, elbows touching mat,
and face grazing the earth-dirt floor.

Sangoma, Ngomo says, *Doctor man. Doctor good.*
And begins translating ingredients in the remedies
his thick fingers are picking out – *Bark. Mix seeds.*
Cameras flash. *This, leaves. Crush.* Fingers rubbing
black powder. *Is herbs. Dry in fire. Using for heads.*
More flash. *These insect. Mixing in blood. Hens.*
And, suddenly inaction, followed by lowing moans.

Then the doorway darkens again: two indistinct
shapes lope in, stand still until a drum knocks up
its rhythmic drive that has the pair gyrating with
nifty footwork, arms snaking, and heads bobbing –
no eye contact again – the dance rising to climax
accompanied by jangling bangles at ankles and
wrists. Then collapsing quiet as an off-white bowl
crosses the floor. *Is gifts,* Ngomo says. *You Zulu,
you bring hens. Is traditional.*

Yes, traditional.
Like the plastic cartons and jars holding the potions;
the tin-lids thinned into bangles; the ice-cream tub
for tips. Cameras flash. Trickling rands through
fingers, we sidle our leave.

Outside, the sun glares down.
Red kites wheel. The music bangs out its spell again.
Our heads begin to spin.

Waiting On

Precious her name-label says:
her eyes, big, brown
the whites already yellowing.

Bigger, her earrings –
silver hoops that loop
from lobes almost to shoulder.

And breasts? Well, you guessed –
cupped handfuls like melons:
big, bigger, biggest.

And as she sashays away
to bring us coffee,
her hips roll in liquid rhythm.

It's a dismissal of sorts:
her blackness
outclassing our white.

Outside, framed by cloud-white skies,
kites are circling: black silhouettes
drifting on thermals.

More waiting on –
for another dismissal –
just as precious, you bet.

Zulu Dancing

Though his loose-limbed rhythmic saunter
lends his head a dismissive arrogance bordering
on insubordination, that instance dwindles
into insignificance once the music has kicked in:

then the plagal cadences, the bitter shrill whistling,
the chants, and the tam-tam's battering thwack
have him zigzagging angular in some hand-me-down
tribal memory of the battle challenge's aggressive

jaggedness, as spraunged on haunches, with knees
at ninety degrees, he's jabbing and stabbing
at air, eyes ablaze in outstaring glare, or rolling
crazily in some Zulu juju – a frenzy possessing

his lifted foot, shifting it, high, higher, then slapping
flat against the ground, again after again, his lissom body
glistening in dressings of sweat, his black skin toning
to gold with more agogic mockery till feigning defeat

like a wounded animal in a ground-circling,
limb-lagging sadness – only to leap to a final
jab-stabbing attack – foot-slap, stab, jab, stab

and our awed, gormless, lost-for-words applause

while, all the time, his driver stands having a smoke
outside, and fixing new gigs on his mobile phone.

Impala

Have a languid demeanour –
slow, nonchalant, delicate,
their movement liquid,
almost indiscernible

like their form's content:
shape balanced against shape,
and shaded as if pieced together
from marquetry.

Could outstare you
if they really needed to,
but are gracious, lithe,
dignified

so wait for you to go
like hotel room-maids –
for, after all,
this is their homeland.

Kudu

Look at you suspiciously
giving you the voodoo gaze
interrogating your face
reading your eyes.

Are not unnerved initially –
almost as though they expect
you to come up with
the right password
before they can let you
into their territory, their world.

But it's you that's flustered –
overawed by their presence,
their caramel-amber beauty
flushed under full sunlight – so
fumbling for camera, binocs
can only come up with *Wow*.

It's that that flummoxes them,
distresses – and off they duck,
legs bucking, into the forest-dark,
their amber collapsing to blue-black

under low tree canopy and
the uncertainties
of chance meetings.

Duiker

Hide shyly in bushland scrub,
the dark thickets
of shrubby undergrowth.

Only splinters of light
glimmering on eye-whites
betray their presences.

Once seen, give you the once-over
with their doe-eyed surprise, then push
nudging away, legs lifting delicately,
mincing and tripping through darkness

melt into invisibility.

(Is it mankind they fear
with his stunning gun ? ...   )

But distanced from road and track,
become bolder, come out into the open.

Then their coats glow cinnamon-ginger,
almost a lingering burnished red
bright and vulnerable under full sun –
but stay, grazing,
slowly zig-zagging their route
to the future.

Young Buffalo

is a puzzling conundrum.

Face to face returns your stare,
unfazed – a gaze that knows
no concession – just a bland
deadly-factual, matter-of-fact
absence of any sort of emotion,
a couldn't-carelessness:
an Ama-bovvered attitude.

But inside his haunches
there linger the rhythms he's been
handed down: that lymph-pumping
rush of muscle, blood and bone
locked within darkness, a bubbling
cauldron that any moment could
overspill, but for the now is content
with a head tossing, a dismissive
snort, and slight forward trot

till, stopping short at the egret's
question mark,

resorts to out-staring again
in a containment of sorts.

Shooting Rhino

i.m. Martin Booth (1944-2004)

You're aware keratin's the carrot dragging
your attention, so it's patience, and a steady hand
you need, especially when he's doing that wheeling
heave, coming in and out of focus, and in again
in his quiet grazing, a delicate swiping of grass, ·
a stumbling, halting stroll that counterpoints his bulk.

The trick's lining him up in your sights –
that's if you can distinguish him from the crop
of rock just under the tree-line, that black mass
which looks as if it's grazing, head down, and rump
declining to ground level.

So it's sharp binoculars you need – and luck – once
you've spotted him, bringing him into focus.
Full view. Centred, so he occupies the total scan:
a magnificent pan of a magnificent animal:
> *Black rhino. Adult bull. Three years old.*

What sheer bulk of hulking flesh. If you were a painter
you'd break him down to planes and plates, make the play
of light define his flanks, chart the massy anvil of his head,
that almost excuse for an eye so small against the jaw-line,
his pricked-up ears, and those curving thorns of horn:
> *No wonder horn commands high prices.*

And you need to take his horns, so bring him in big, bigger
till you can see his ears' whiskery bristles, his twitching tail,
the way the dung has dried on his hide, the spittle dribbling
on his slow rolling lips, and the defiant spikes that make him
wanted. Vulnerable.

And you're getting him large, larger, in your sights –
till he's practically in your face, has taken hold of your mind,
his horns thorning in your head, and you're falling down
your sight-line, falling into him
but are ready with that finger-itching readiness
and clicking – once – twice –
have him bagged:

a gap filled in the family album.

In 1986 Martin Booth, poet and writer, visited Luanga National Park in Zambia
to survey the area for a television documentary centring on a group of "upwards
of thirty" black rhino. Returning in September 1987 with a film crew, he found
that the particular group of black rhino had been reduced to "perhaps three."

Elephant Sighting

No way elegant, alighting on the pile
of curry-coloured dung, so freshly-left
it's still steaming, that suggests they can't
be far away – a fact confirmed by scars
of twigs and disfigured branch that map
their ziggurats of progress.

Inside the safari-jeep
anticipation grows palpable,
fingers twitching to binoculars,
cameras handy,
as we climb higher, inching
gingerly, gears taking the strain,
through scrub, rock and bush, the engine
ticking and purring until we reach the hill-top,
the sky a vast caul, sun riding high,
landscape an unrolled blanket
with its rise and fall like waves,
its hill-tops crested with trees.

And there, down below,
half-visible, unhassled,
this stately galleon of bull elephant,
slowly rolling through bush
in a ponderous, unruffled saunter
like a Sunday afternoon stroll,
getting on with the business of living,
his trunk pulling and twisting at leaves, twigs,
thin branches and stuffing them into
pink lips, his whip-tail flailing, and flap ears
twitching nervously, on the alert,
his seed of an eye, shining wetly –

And then, alarm –
and a jolt into a jogging trot –
a nimbleness out of kilter with his weight
that takes him right out of sight.

Nile Crocodiles

That sly variety with slits for eyes
riding high on headsides,
and a mean grin that levers to a metre wide
revealing files of teeth, needle-fine
like rip-saws.

Feigning nonchalance,
lie log-like, doggo,
sunning selves on river-banks,
and trying not to be there.

Or, in water,
float without motion,
then sink, sink,
silently.

Always eyes tightly open,
their wet lens jetting shut
with a camera-flick

but it's more than images they take.

Though can go for days without food,
are eager to seize what's offered –
snaffle it, and twist, thrashing and snatching
till off flesh comes in bloody chunks –
then guzzle-gulp.
Can manage chickens whole.

King of Umfolizi's River system,
men in white are apprising
why tocsins have their hook
in their food chain
so bringing their decline –
the minutes ticking
their future away

most of their hatchlings
never growing up,
like Peter Pan.

Tooth

for Wendy Jones

No molar this:
is a render, a tearer,
a tusk.

Held tentatively
resting in the palm –
nearly two feet of bone.

And curved like a scimitar grimace
with striations of stain
from ivory white
graining through to ochre at its tip
underwritten with the insignia
of years of chomping herbage.

And so heavy
that on receiving it
the hand sinks.

But then you'd expect as much
from something that's apparently
clumsy on land
and not too happy in water –
and yet can outrun
a man.

No wonder crocs are chary:
this knife-slice descending
can snap a crocodile spine
in two.

What might
within a single strike.

Thank God, thank Christ, thank Darwin
hippos are vegetarian.

African Wild Dogs

With pelts the tan, brown, cream
of cast-off furs in Oxfam shops
they look, at best, as if they've had
a bad dye-hair day at the hairdresser's
and the colours have run, making them
patchy-flashy, smudged.

Their outlines blurred,
their intent disguised
only their black-tipped Micky-Mouse ears
tell of arrival.
The remainder comes hard on heel
                        down at mouth
                        tongue lolling, panting
                        tail lagging   an afterthought.

Scions of a lean eating-machine
managed by practice and need,
they centre from the edge of things:
                        yesterday's wonders
                        today's ambiguities
                        tomorrow's perhapses.

Like distant cousins at family funerals
they mouth ready platitudes.

Their wake is getting a skinful.
Their mourning, skin-deep.
Their memorial, a mass of bones.

Vultures

don't make any bones about the fact
their ugly-beauty underscores
the deaths they celebrate
as wheeling overhead
their wingspans, black against sun,
announce the quick of things
is coming to a gristly end.

So sit flat-packed in jacarandas,
grey-shawled, waiting,
their heads like butcher's hooks,
eyes a gimlet
overseeing the accidents
of life.

Till rattling into action,
shoulders lowered in a bank-teller's
stoop, go hopping with a flopping
bounce, a dragging wing-flapping step
by stop that's revamped into stamping dance
like clowns trampling their pants down,
and trying to free their feet
from what they've just stumbled into.

And yet are deadly serious:

though ace at meeting death
head on
steer clear of hyenas
congregating   circling

just out of reach.

Hyena

Skulking among vultures
in his moth-eaten combats
the way he slopes back on his back heels
seems for all the world
as if he's trying hard to stop
his insides from sliding out
of his backside.

That's why his face
has that grinning grimace
   its yellow clenched teeth
   its snarl
   its glaring stare of pain
from the strain
of hanging on, hanging on

for the grim death
he's so well and truly
rehearsed in.

Understanding Dung Beetles

They come bumbling at you – head height,
so you have to duck – black whizzing bullets
streaking arrow straight at speed, then go arcing
in to land, and begin their trundling toil.

It's their sensitive sense of smell
that delivers them to hunted dung,
and capturing it, have to secrete it,
rolling it to safety, and burial.

They work arse-over heels, literally:
though have spade-shaped heads
use their hind legs to shift a dung ball
fifty times their body weight: backwards.

Make their mating places underground,
laying their eggs in these rich dumps of muck,
larders for the larvae's birthing girth.

Get all their nutrients from dung:
squeeze and suck the seeps of liquid,
rich in feeding.

Scientists calculate they navigate
via polarisation patterns of planet;
and some governments fine drivers
for crushing them to scabby pulp.

> (There's foresight for you -
> putting dung-shovellers before cars.)

Dung is all they own.
Get high on piles of ordure.

And dedicating their lives to dung
question the testament
that bread is the staff of life.

Get the Picture

For Elaine & Graham

Floppy sun-hatted
Graham and Elaine are off out again –
third time today –
tripoded camera with fast action flash,
extending lens for close-ups,
and binocs for getting things focussed.

Have a handy bag
stashed with books on birds –
hers a trim, slim guide;
his fatter;
and a note book
for writing down sightings.

Are gadgety-happy:
back in their hotel room
set up a laptop
that translates the snaps they take
into templates for sketches
they overscore in water-colour
to make a holiday journal of sorts,
dated and named:
S. Africa, November '09.

Know all along
what matters most
is having things in perspective.

Forest Walk, *St Lucia, South Africa*

Gert's escorting us
identifying strangling vines
that squeeze trees hollow, dead;

bracket fungus, like whitish china, that's edible;
or glossier orange that's not;

and birds:
  crested turacos, escapees from *The Night Garden*;
  butcher shrikes that spike their victims on twigs;
  yellow weavers with inverted nest-entrances;

more birds:
  the red-throated, azure-spotted,
  green-backed, purple-barred,
  pink-fronted, white-eyed,
  black-tailed etceteras
(you'd be forgiven for thinking he's invented their names).

Not so the scratched leopard tracks
on its claw-scoring tree we saw those

or the spiral-horned kudu buck no mistaking him

and the male croc
threshing head and tail
way out in the estuary
in courtship ritual
at Honeymoon Bend gets full marks for irony

and the stuttering butterfly
striped white and black
with amber-yellowy flash
that, time after time,
we tried so hard to photograph.

Yes, like so many opportunities:
seen, but not taken.

Question of Facts

Zander catalogues actualities:

mammals	five hundred species
reptiles	15 varieties, of which 100 snakes
birds	326 types
insects	thousands, with many yet to be named

Knows where roam, make their home
     Where/when/how/why they thrive

Relishes the pleasure of   black mambas
                       dune adders
                       rhombic egg snakes
                       the whistling frog

Can tell you where/when the leopard prowls

Understands   bloodbonds of crocodiles
                       pack-trackings of African wild-dogs
                       gene-pools of hippos
                       matings of toads

Knows all there is to know
About biodiversity, animal taxonomya
Sets great store by sex

Ask the wife
She knows he knows
Can see it in his limpid eyes
         his liquid fingers

Jeep Safari, Night Sitting

We're out in the safari jeep
ten of us, game-spotters,
under the vast canopy
of the southern night sky,
stars scattered like salt
from heaven's salt-mill.

Trevor has the lamp,
arcing it over St. Lucia's Wetlands Park
in pans of light - grey-green pools at distance –
that ghost over foliage and brush up against
the treeline, the grass clumps,
cut-down pine-tree stumps,
the safari palms
trying to find sightings –
rhino, nightjar, kudu,
bush buck, duiker, buffalo –
in fact, anything we may or may not already have seen.

Isolated in seas of darkness
save where Trevor's lamp invades,
pins of light wink, blinking back.

There's a clear division in the darkness,
ebony brushed by the moon,
and though no ground is being given,
nothing substantial gained,
the motion is being carried.
The parliament of animals have decided
the eyes have it.

(And keep it tonight they will ...)

Limited Editions, South Africa

Black and white sizable linocuts
limited to six prints in a run of six issues each,
each numbered out of six at left hand corner
and signed at bottom right;
designed by Wetlands Native Artists
to raise funds for cultural needs;
and limited to two subjects:
one, animals; the other, resettlement.

You can see where the tools have been
nicking, cutting, slicing, scoring, chipping away
to reveal reverse images as simply-bold
as those cave-paintings
from pre-historic times
we've seen up country:
black standing out against white.

Two we pick depicting animals –
they're for our grandkids' nursery walls:
 on one, hippo, elephant, impala, croc
 graze peaceably together;
 on the other, black buffalo and white rhino
 drink side by side at the water hole.

Those depicting resettlement
 nicking, cutting, slicing, scoring, chipping away
 in reverse image
 to reveal blacks being helped into vans,
 fires dowsed, huts pulled down
 white overseers in profile
 with batons, guns, and machetes to hand
 sizable, designed, simply-bold

        black standing out against white
we push to one side as unacceptable.

For, after all,
getting the present you deserve
has been since pre-historical times
a matter of choice between limited editions.
in art, in politics.

Bedazzled

The slatted backs
      of a herd of upright teak sun chairs
           legs spread-eagled and at grass
               among grazing angled sun-loungers

      camouflaged under low palms
      huge hands of ferns
      and big, spreading cycads

          set against a midground
        of sun-blessed decking
    with diagonals and horizontals
patterning the ground in stripes

      and foregrounded verticals
      of the balcony fence

        conspire to remind us
        that the collective noun for zebra
        is not a herd
        but a dazzle

X Factor

X marks   the spot on the picture-postcard
of St Lucia, South Africa
we send to the grandkids
telling them we've arrived safely
while giving them a Geography lesson
on the q t

X marks   the location of the British dead
on the map-plan of the Battle of Isandhlwana
and brought into clearer focus
when we visit the white-piled cairns
pocking the ground

X marks   the stains left behind on the shower wall
when in the battle with hotel invaders
we zapped the last cockroaches

X marks   the "Excellent" box on the questionnaire
of Brenda, our holiday rep, –
every time, everywhere

not to mention the kisses
x and x
she deals out like sweets to kids
on our cheeks
the day we leave

Fringe Benefits

Egyptian Lizard

Finger-thin splinter
of lemon, emerald and black
zipping back and flank together

this lizard is magician:
vanishes without giving
you a chance

to register his presence.
His eyes have that manic
flashing gaze of panicky sheep

and his head that sheep-chiselled
shape as if it's just been made
and he's surprised he's been able

to catch a likeness at all.
His hands possess
the self-same skin pinkiness

of the fingers of a new-born child,
flexing for possession
And his tail's a flail

where he whips himself
to vacancies again:
gone before he's here.

Felucca Crossing

For Hemant, Min and Eileen

I   It's something to do with the grace
and dignity of felucca diagonals
that attracts – like the sidling approach
that Luxor street vendors use – that slanting
angle from kerb/wall/road:
Yo wan felucca.

And there's elegance, too,
despite their soiled galabeyas the colour
of sails, their grime-filled nails and sticky hands
with inside pink fingers, their dirt-chafed heels –
as targeting you, they lean, angling
to catch your glance in a sort of magnetism:
Yo wan felucca –
Not a question, more a suggestion, a fact.

II   *Fe luc ca.* How it chimes:
three syllables defining a curriculum for living
of this Nubian three-man crew.

And not simply a lesson in mathematics:
the geometry of the two lateen sails,
diagonal, angled and triangling
with yard and tautened rope
so that one sitting at the tiller, plus one at boom, one at sail
equals more than the sum of water and wind.

And not the principles of physics, either:
like the properties of motion, the action of pulleys,

rudder and rope, the fulcrum-pull of muscle
or letting the current take the strain
to reckon the displacement of water
and prove a theorem of movement.

But the rhythms of history,
its courtesies and customs, codes of tradition,
the unspoken nudgings of blood -
intuitive and inborn - that spawn the haul of rope,
tease of tiller, ease of boom
to that stately pace, almost weightless,
sailing through the river's click and pluck
in the slow, zig-zagging tack from bank to bank
of the forty-minute jaunt upstream

and that uncompromised downstream ten-minute glide,
the wind in full sail, prow knifing the Nile
as crossing to the Valley of the Kings
and back to earth again.

Red Sea Snorkelling

The pull of the moon's haul – gently,
gently – rocking the sea to mother-tapped cradle,
the waves bussing the shoreline
with their pluck and splosh,
their insistent conspiratorial sibilants.

And deeping beneath the sea's veneered
meniscus I see fish.
                    More fish. Fish
hanging in an under-water curtain-swirl, a falling
of gauze, wrapping back in on themselves, fold
on fold, rising and sinking, streamlining
all ways, and spiralling, circle within circle –
a flotilla of colour, gawping soundlessly
and suspended like a child's nursery-mobile
but water-borne, stringless.

Such a gallimaufry of gaudy baubles –
the stuff Tiffany would have drafted into glass –
their dull mulberry turning as they turn
to purples burnished with bronze, or etched
with lip- and eye-liners in turquoise, emerald,
pink, amethyst and aquamarine
all silently gliding, turn-tail-turning
as if they've been scooped up and gently bent
almost in half, and put back again,
some striped finely in orange and black,
some patchy amber and white, as the sunlight
is angled, refracting through the gin-clear water
and dappling the sea-bed in reflected skeins
like the skeins of other fish self-reflecting
in zebra stripes, the coral beneath
shadowing their progress.

And the thin-as-pencil fish with thinner heads
snout-like, their tessellated scales glistening to lemon-yellow
and silvery-zipped, opalescent under submarine sunshine
and making translucent their blood pulse, their lymph
and all their inside workings
machining away at living, tick after tick,
but silently in the stilled watery depths.

This – and this. And this,
the sea's munificence surpassing mere attractiveness
and advancing beyond the simply visual
towards the magical.

Fins, gills and tail on hold
or patiently hushing them forward
in their turns, their whorls
to make draping veils trailing around legs
in a blessing of sharing nearness
as with their Mick Jagger lips, their Bardot pout
they meet me practically face to face,
their eye-contact iris-lighting
as if recognising
another of the world's creature-sons.

Mr 10%, *Hotel Fort Arabesque*, Hurghada

arrives daily, sporting his shirt-name *Fox*,
though in this complex of alternatives
he's actually called Mohammed (too many of them).
Coal-black, his chipped teeth tarred, he sells us
massages – with *Commission*. He has to touch.
Slaps hands. Makes high fives as readily as his smiles.

Can read our lethargy. Though "indolence"
doesn't enter his word-book. He's smart. And knows it.
Lubly jubly. Ma fren. You like. Is good.
Works the hotel beach hard, his body-splash
and pidgin English filling the air after he's gone.
Understands how vast the gap between his words
and the Thai girls' hand-on experience,
their more than 60% fingering. Their silent tongue.

Between the falcon and the fox

The falcon soaring, banking and
dipping in a twist, to level out, stalling
like a child's paper-plane, and
dropping – an innocence – to land
a settling rest on the Aswan-stone parapet
of the copy-cat Arabic fort (almost cut-out
balsa-wood in certain uncertain lights),
his seed-eye wide-bright in slitted
wadjet-shape, and fixed on survival

The dog-fox trotting across
the seven o'clock morning lawn,
side-sliding in that mix of hesitant
delicacy and purposeful spurt – but
stately, dignified – and stopping
to sniff at the water-sprinkler,
and sipping a drink from the water-sprinkler,
his flap-ears aligned
in the outline of his jackal animus

And in the grounds of this hotel complex
between the falcon and the fox
        Horus and Anubis
lie the holiday-makers
taking the best of the sun
till the jestings of death

Hotel Fort Arabesque, Makadi Bay, Egypt

Egyptian fox, not collectable

Not the Beswick pottery-ware Reynard –
picture-book look of a fox,
clean-limbed, almost in dress-coat
with his laundered bib and tucker

so you half expect a dickey-bow,
his pelt wearing a reddy glow,
ears pricked, tipped out in black,
and that curved bush

of tail topped with shotted darkness
and white, his eyes amber-bright,
and almost a sly, inviting smile
slicing his chiselled snout –

Not that, but this scrawny
marauding swiftness that slides besides
the manicured hedge, scrabbles
the gap, stands Anubis-still

till settles for daring, makes a dash
for it, his mangy flank's sandiness
almost patchwork in the thin Egyptian
light, as dancing across open grass

in a cross between gallop and trot,
with an underness of stealth,
a suggestion almost that he knows
he's trespassing – but makes the safety

of the grove of young royal palms
(fronds silvering in the off-shore breeze),
the oleander's waxy leaves reflecting
effortlessly, and the bougainvillea

luxuriating in its cherry-reds, its raspberry,
and whites – makes this his haven-oasis,
close to the sprinkler tap the Nubian
groundsman (never admitted inside

the hotel accommodation)
leaves drizzling for him.
No. Not collectable.
Not him.

This Need of Foxes

Woke to a distant howling
of foxes, their calls in antiphon
ringing through the night:

a mournful, hollow yawp –
nothing sharp, nothing yelpish
but a lowing, not like sheep, not mongrel

but in a need, a moaning desire
as if put apart and aching to be complete
in the stark grandeur of the dark,

the moon solemnly opulent,
the stars a spilt spangling
in the night-time's darkness:

and that call – a bottomless emptiness,
a yearning, as if to say that the earth's
turning is but ceremony of celebration

of all that is, all that has been,
and this dog-fox, this vixen are its heralds
slipping through shrubbery and undergrowth,

their terracotta pelt with welted black
on their backs and the backs of their shanks,
their tails clubbed with bobbled white shock

marking their progress as slowing to a check,
a turn, and – flash – a lolloping that has them
strides ahead of selves before they've

started, then stopping to throw
aloft that long cockerel-crow of a moan
announcing you have to accept

we are here
so hear us, hear us, hear
our long yearning howl:

this need of foxes coming together
in that awareness of being,
that continuing, which is our us

Of perfection

The Nubian bar-staff – lads to a man –
stand behind their maroon and tan uniforms
and eye up and down the frauleins, mademoiselles,
the English girls.

Never so much female flesh seen before this season:
sheer perfection.

How their eyes climb glaciers of backs,
                abseil cliffs of shoulders,
                chasm down cleavages,
                slide past temples of plenty,
                tombs of wombs,
then drop anchor at pubic deltas:
sheer perfection.

And how – the whites of their eyes already yellowing –
they save their face behind practised smiles
as wide as the Nile

then melt away
to the store-room behind the bar
where, getting a grip on things,
they begin to bring themselves to perfection.

Aswan, Egypt

Hunting Wild

African-eyed like sad cows
he has left Morocco.
There are no date palms in London,
no camels bearing loads,
and flies are not so busy here.

Though hashish is bartered
in back street deals, alcohol freely spills
and women wear faces in public:
he cannot unhook his looks from their lips.

Westernized, he grows rings on his wedding finger.
But, at night, dreams of the friendship of lads,
white midday suns, opaline skies
and cool winds freshening over dunes.

In this new Mecca
though he has relinquished the old gods,
how he misses the call
of the muezzin in the minaret.
He cannot stop his gaze turning
to the East.

Innocent as his olive skin,
he is not old enough to understand
societies have separate addictions,
or that Truth slides and wrinkles
like youthful looks.

For the now, he knows these absolutes:
the arrogance of loneliness,
the openness of need.

Fringe Benefits, India

We've watched the carpet-makers paraded out under
the awning's shade for this morning's loom-display –
a handful of men holding in their heads and hands
the intricate designs of coloured wools that constitute
these jewels of rugs passed down the generations –
have seen the burnishings of back, the separation
of threads, the lavings and the shearing-snip; and now
we're grouped to view the combing-smooth.

I've seen all this before in Turkey but suddenly notice
the single woman working in the weaving-shed her face
lifting to snatch a glance at us. Caught off guard,
her doe-eyes focussing slowly on my face, she smiles
a child-like smile – the sort that melts all injury away –
seems for all the world like my Mum busy at her stitchery.
But, squatting on her heels, sari cowling her jet hair, knotting
the warp and weft of threads almost invisible in her slipping
fingers and slickly plaiting into fringe the stringlike tassels
valueless in comparison with the carpet's patterned weave,
she's doing things my mother never needed to.

Having eez fringe benefits the salesman quips, his teeth
gleaming through the managed laughter hanging on his lips.
But can be leaving off. Eez all same. No extra pay.
Or keeping them. All same. Hearing his pidgin English,
her eyes narrow into slits; her head bends back to work,
her fingers knitting at the threads while we cross the yard
to the carpet saleroom. Once we're seated, rum-and-coked,
the salesman's reached top-gear: *These beauty of riches past*
can be keeping. Make specially for us. Though we notice
as the carpets bellow out there's barely a fringe on show.

.

Half an hour of salesman's patter later, we're outside
once more: no weavers at the looms, no fringing woman
but, screened partially from public view, a garage-wallah
caressing a sleek Mercedes that's defiantly brand-new.
These beauty can be keeping ... or leaving off ... no extra
pay ... specially for us ... eez all same ... eez fringe benefits

A Week In Bangkok

I   Skeins of sandalwood in the temple
the susurration of monks at prayers
saffron and orange their robes

II   The tintinnabulation of bells – bright, stark –
ringing down the wind

III   Candles – many candles – in glass
their flickerings reflecting on the stretched limbs
of the golden Buddha
his jewel eyes

IV   In the water garden
under the haze of daylong sunlight
taking the lotus-flower
long-stemmed from water
and folding it
petal on petal
in translucent waxness
more paper thin than paper

V   At nightfall
the cicadas tzinging down by the river
late birds calling
and strands of dance music
counterpointing the jig of neon
with tides of workers –
ferry after ferry – returning home

VI   From high-rise blocks
the drift and glimmer of lit charcoal
thud of doors

thud of lifts
and raised voices
ringing down hollow corridors

VII   Amid the city throb
with its thronging population
its traffic snarl
      the tuk-tuk's splutter
      and monorails' shuttle
the loneliness of knowing
only the consolation
of being alone

Ironies More Than Orange

Dong Minh Man tells us about the Cu Chi tunnel system

He's usually straight-faced, almost bland, as he negotiates
the pitfalls of English grammar, unaware of how the consonants
lay their traps for him, but, today, his face brightens into lantern:
eyes lively, eyebrows dancing, his mouth, lips, tongue
rehearsing the mantra he's rehearsed from childhood:

> The American they fire the babies
> fire the children   the woman
> fire cows   other animal
> They fire the Buddha even
>
> They burn the house   the crop   burn trees
> Take their leaves   their fruits   burn them
> The American they burn them
>
> They bomb   poison water   poison the river
> Spray chemical   you know agent orange
> flame napalm   the ground all burn   no grow rice
> Our family wasted   gone still now born unformed
> in the second   the third generation
>
> But the trees leafs back again
> The mangrove   the rubber   the bamboo
> they grow   their leaf they thick and strong
> They fruit four season   many fruit
>
> Our people farmer by day   soldier in night
> They dig pit   make swing-trap
> American they step   and swish it spin
> They fall in bamboo spike kill him   he die

Some soldier of our   they live ten eleven year
under the ground dig deep three level
Dig tunnel tunnel very dark   No no light

Have men and woman keep separate
Have like hospital you know under the ground
Have escape to keep safe

But all no stay alive   they die

Our soldier secret know only three thing

walk without trace   turn many leafs to hide
cook without smoke   give morning mist be brother to the smoke
talk without speak   teach fingers to walk words

Falling silent, his eyes deepen to grievances.

Forty years on, he understands the ironies that lie
in clichés such as actions speak louder than words
and the future's bright, the future's orange.

Suon's weekly English class, Cambodia

I   Cycling the potholed road to Seng Balin's house
this five o'clock dawning, what Suon warms to
is the apricot blush of sunlight hazing the skyline.

    Amazed at the landscape's return to ordinariness
he relishes the natural scheme of things as peddling by
lotus beds their green shafts lancing through plates

    of leaf and pink breaking bud; girls river-washing;
lads emptying wicker fish-traps; then on past insect nets,
spaced out like flags, catching crickets for market;

    skirting mango grove and hardwoods; and biking through
the huts stilted above water and woven from osier and
palm; and on into Balin's yard, the household shrine,

    scattering his leggy hens, and up the rough-hewn ladder
angling to platformed veranda, till sitting, sipping green tea,
around the charcoal stove …

II   In good time, they're going through those phrases
he's already pored over, day after day, as challenging self
to master adverbs of manner or place in his father's primer,
and mouthing aloud those word-lists he's practised:
the sound traps of dough, cough, rough, bough, through;
the hard and soft "g" in rogue, rouge, garage, language.

    As for verbs, while he's keen to reach the future perfect,
he's troubled enough by the present tense, not to mention
the historic and those past participles: shoot into shot,
lose to lost, keep to kept, go to went …

And nouns? Though he can't see much sense bringing
down to earth polysyllables like intellectual, academic
or even political potential*, he's come to terms with
scatterings of mother, father, brother, uncle and
their relationship. But that's only to be expected.

Being teachers of English, his father, brother, uncle
were shot, and his mother lost, so he's keen to retrieve
what's been kept, what they went through:
the language of forbidden family.

Postcard from Beijing

Hotel's massive – bars, gym, sauna,
shops, massage - "evlything yu wan" —
so no need to go out. Saves crossing
the eight lanes of traffic, both ways.
Besides, have seen Tiananmen Square
on TV loadsatimes – bit like their folk:
once seen one, seen 'em all.

Massive? No, gi-normous! I swear
it grows overnight. Just today, eighth
into my trip, found a tenth restaurant –
speciality Greek cuisine! Moussaka with
rice or noodles! Its décor of gold and
black lacquer reminds me how you like
Marmite. Yes. You like *Marmite*!

Room's on thirty-fourth floor. Reckon
it sways, so thought I'd better let you know
how you've missed topping-up your
vertigo. And – you guessed? – the fridge
ticks, the sink drips. All night. The TV
shows old westerns. Listened to re-runs
of **The Magnificent Seven** on and off
through the party-wall all p.m. Done
great guns for my Mandarin.

Not a Hell-hope of losing track of time.
Rugs changed daily in the lifts – silk ones
in cobalt, jade and pink – each day's name
picked out in the yellows of scrambled-egg.

As planned, am staying put, writing-up
my Chinese cycle. Here's the latest:

Each dusk, a waiter
brings dices of ice that clatter
against the sides of his wine bucket.
Dropped it once: said fff-forget it!

Knew that would make you smirk.

Having the life of my time.
Wish you were here: you'd hate it!
    Lurv R

    xxx

Visiting the floating village
on Cambodia's Toule Sap (Great Lake)
and being greeted by a Vietnamese refugee
child

He'd sighted us a while back and zagging
between the maze of floating sheds that
pass as houses, church, and stores has
gradually reached our boat, till, cutting

his own motor, has his skiff drifting tight
alongside. Unfazed by our occidental
looks and obvious wealth – the hats,
the bags, the cameras – he makes a sad

face that out-faces us. *One dollar* his
ritual insists. *One dollar.* Doesn't stretch
out hands, but unwraps the python he's
scarved around his arms and neck, and

grasping it just short of chiselled head
waggles it. Left. Right. Waggles more,
making its camouflage patches flash
under glancing sunlight. Left. Right.

No hiss. *One dollar* he persists. *One dollar.*
He shares the snake's blandness, his own
snake-eyes fixed till they become quick
at sight of cash. Sad-faced still, he pockets

the dollar, and turns swiftly away to let rip
the outboard motor, zipping his craft to other
passers-by. With luck they'll find his smile,
and place the snake greenbacks nearer liberty.

Halkidiki Nonet

I   *Dawn Flight*

Sea of clouds, as grey as Atlantic waves,
stretching beneath us to cloud-outcrops
like knobby rocks or curly copse
on island shorelines ...

The horizon cloud-line vermilion-tinged,
shading away, as sun breaks, to orange
through apricot, then pink ...

And, over-arching, a cowl
of aquamarine-cum-turquoise, with slivers
of silver like scratched slicks on backs
of mirror-glass – the whole skyscape open,
clear and vast as a Dali surreal painting ...

And, yes, it is surreal
our flying so high
with no strings attached ...

II *Another Country*

Where there were hundreds
upon hundreds of olive trees
colonading down hillsides to the Aegean,
> grey-green leaves defined by diadems of berry,
> trunks lopped, and branches rounded to copse,
> the long rows echoing the dip and
> rise of the land, its contours, its bones
there is now a building-site with workmen
stripped to singlets among ziggurats of brick,
concrete blocks, plinths and lintels;
pyramids of earth; rucks of fractured pan-tiles
mixed with shattered plasterboard;
and the everywhereness of pallet
and polythene sheeting

and just five olive trees, kept for their looks,
> trunks pruned to clean-lined-sheen, limbs lissom,
> everything trimmed to aesthetics
> except their black-brown fruit
> bruised underfoot like sheep-dung:

all the rhythms of history, of farming
seduced by the pizzazz of design, the razzmatazz of tourism,

and the past translated to another country.

III *Greek Holiday Complex*

Multi-million pound investment,
architect-planned and built on landscaped hillside,
with olive groves cleared
except for token specimens
as concession to history ...

Beneath cream parasols
ranks of rattan sunbeds,
tables between with blue eyes of ashtrays ...

Kidney-shaped pools, pale-blue-cool
and set in cream paving that sashays
diagonally to the Aegean –
all angles compromised
by the line of the horizon ...

The blues of the sea, blues of the pools,
and the cream gradations on exteriors
balanced by interior décor of creams
and of blues, with the occasional white flash
in pots, robe and stripe ...

Few Greeks – none holidaying – and the staff,
all under thirty, drafted in from Macedonia, Latvia,
Slovenia, Poland, Romania, Serbia, Ukraine,
Estonia, et cetera, et cetera –
all orders placed in English ...

The buildings not yet three years' old
and already the writing is on the wall
and – you guessed? – in English.
It orders: *Happy New Fear.*

IV   *Woodworm*

The Greek sun leaning on our heads,
we'd ambled past the pink and white oleanders,
up the dust-track, the fields shorn to stubble,
and everywhere walls stalking the hillside –
Built, Jill said, *by Albanian immigrants.*
Skilled workers in stone. Cheap labour –
past pistachio, fig-tree, and olive going to nothing,
and on up the hill, round bends, past side-roads
to the old wind-mill.

Stavros greeted us, proud of his thirty-year
resurrection of his granddad's bequest: new floorboards
and hand-rail, replaced drive-spindle and gear,
fresh white-limed querns and exterior, beams restored
and varnished, the new sails – and listened
to Geoff, expert-on-everything, rabbiting on about
death-watch beetle and woodworm, then borrowing biro
to write down his Cuprinol wisdom: *Will kill it, kill it all.*

Back at out hotel, we're greeted graciously by Eva,
cheap Romanian waitress – cheaper with her fellow countryman,
skilled in the kitchen, and cheaper still than Greek youth
wanting more than kitchen work, waiting on, wall-building -
Eva saved from entering the western slave-market trade,
the night-girl grooming, but having eyes on chancing
a passage to Canada to resurrect her future, so for the time being
is satisfied serving **Alpha** beer to Alpha males, and borrowing
our biro to bill us all: *You now pay. Sign. Sign please, sign.*

Oh woodworm. Woodworm:
Pox of commerce, and Geoffrey.
Kill it. Kill it all.

V   *New Gods For Old*

Today, can't make out Mount Olympus:
sky overcast, grey, with only a slash
of sunlight like a knife-blade ripping
through canvas – almost painterly –
its diagonals of light angling away,
and, beneath, in a pool of gold
on the gunmetalled sea – could be burnished –
a fishing boat – it might be Paul's
bringing good news to Corinth.

VI *Similar Differences*

Cosmin, our Romanian waiter,
reminds me of that feral black kitten
that patrols the hotel gardens:
        his dark, gypsy looks
        the way he fixes his gaze,
           then comes running
           as if pleased to see us

        his square, open face
        the way his mouth droops, yaws,
           then breaks into sound
           till we work out his meaning

These differences, though:
        one, his dark-brown eyes, not grey-green
        two, not letting guests
        come close enough to stroke him
        and three, he doesn't scoff
     but pockets our offerings.

Valentino's Aquaclasses
                    for Women of Mixed Nationality

Twelve of them (most old enough to be his grandma)
lend themselves daily at ten to the pool's chill thrill.
Here the Italian slip of a lad pits them to fitness
under the Greek sun's holiday eye: they're saving their youth.

ein zwei drei vier fünf sechs sieben acht

Mye bu-tee-full wiman he shrills from the water,
cam to mee. His glistening figure jigs to the music's
racing bass – slipping slapping flipping flapping clapping hands –
as he restirs the youth in their limbs.

    un deux trois quatre cinque six sept huit

They're locked to his shock of cropped black hair, his knifing smile
as he stretches them – in out / up down / forward back.
His thin eyes pin them. He's limber; they lumber.

    one two three four five six seven eight

Nut-brown, neat-limbed, flat chested, balletic: he's blade of a youth.
They're veritable feasts: melon-breasted, white thighs of Gorgonzola fold
hams of arms, and heads hennaed and permed
more than the hue and curl of their youth.

    uno due tre quatro cinque sei sette otto

By day, they love him like their sons, ride his jibes, feign dismay;
but, at night in the silent films of their dreams see their own
Valentinos rudolfing in silk, stretching wide their thighs – in out in.

He, by day, stretches mind to refind them forty years past:
clean-lined, trim-fit as beauty queens, lissom as him;
and at night, saved by the drained pool, he slips between
his lover's silk sheets and the rhythm of keeping his youth.

sei six sei six sei sechs

say *sex sex sex sex*

say *sex*

VIII *Language Classes*

When you have tried
a variety of evening greetings
     Greek: kalispera
     Romanian: buona serra
     Serbian: dobra vece

and the waiting staff
still favour the German girls
               Guten Abend

then you understand
the language of age
               Good Night

IX   *At the end of the day ...*

Pascali has collapsed the battalion
of cream parasols,
like so many silk moths with folded wings
pegged out on the lepidopterist's board.

It's prelude to how we become:
specimens of *homo sapiens*
in the fauna collection of some omniscient God,
fingers itching for fixing-pins ...